A Charm of Finches

A Charm of Finches

poetry by

Suzanne Rogier Marshall

SHANTI ARTS PUBLISHING
BRUNSWICK, MAINE

A Charm of Finches

Published by Shanti Arts Publishing
Interior and cover design by Shanti Arts Designs

Cover image by Alexander Tarasenkov, 2017
(CC BY-SA 4.0)

Shanti Arts LLC
193 Hillside Road
Brunswick, Maine 04011
shantiarts.com

Printed in the United States of America

ISBN: 978-1-956056-35-8 (softcover)

Library of Congress Control Number: 2022935441

for Jim

Contents

Awakening ❧

My furrowed bark grown thick
with winter, worn coat over worn coat,
heavy, grayed, lichen-furred, clutched tight
around my core, I shut out the cold, want to sleep,
but roots, restless in the night, keep stirring,
burrow underground into silt pockets, buried
sand and clay, glacial till—drill down
through darkness, deep fractures, the groans
of shifting earth—feel around each rock,
deeper still,
    beyond the freeze.
            A poem
coiled in my veins, thrumming, thrumming—
snowmelt, thaw, a mud smell—I hear
the soil breathe, loosen its knot, sweet spring
urging through roots through heart
through limbs, bare branches, soft
with sleep—stretch,
    feather the sky.
            A charm
of finches glitters in my arms, their birdsong
wavering like their flight.

I

Along the Edge of the Mad ❧

A tumble-rush, whitewater roar, the river races, mad
as its name, over cobble

and ledge. Kingfisher rattling overhead, I wander
a jumble of boulders beached at its edge—

granite hump-backed, sun-bleached, streaked
in ochre and dun, glint of quartz.

Amid this wild scatter, a rock the shape of my heart—
two lobes tapered to a point,

tumbled, humbled by water, grit, the hone of time,
ground down. Once jagged, sharp,

now weathered, worn smooth. A heart I can hide
in a pocket, hold in my hand.

Migration ❧

Wrapped in wool army blankets, we tumble
from the backseat of Pop's car,
onto this Dakota farm field, corn-stubble
glazed with ice. From a distance, a wild
gabbling swells. Dusk rolls in on storm clouds,
a blizzard of white flurried wings and honks.
Snow geese fill the air, thousands swirling down,
pairs reaching into husk and mud.

Pop shoulders a long-legged spotting scope
to the field's edge, squints, focuses the lens.
On their way south . . . each year . . . this same field.

My sisters, better at doing what we're told,
stand on tiptoe, take turns peering through glass.

But I, caught in wing-whirl and wind—birds
flocking, surging around me—flap
my woolen arms wildly, push against
the half-frozen ground and
fling myself mid-air—
puddle and splash—already swept
into that larger rhythm of leaving
and coming back.

Front Porch ❧

Work shirt and cap on the back of his chair,
the old man settles in, the afternoon sun falling

on his face, bare chest, the pale furrows
of flesh over his belt. Behind him

cordwood, freshly split and stacked, presses
against the house shoulder-high. The man squints

into the distance, leans forward, one foot planted
in summer, the other in the growing dark.

Briar Thicket 🌿

Pop pushes the nurse away, knots his fists.
Piss-ant! Jackass! Trapped in a tangle of dying
brain cells, shriveled cortex, twisted wires and
tubes, he takes a swing, his forearms
scratched and bleeding,

my son, blackberry juice staining his hands,
his mouth, sweet summer smell, wriggles deeper
into places I can't reach,
then the shriek, hornet's nest,
stingers, thorns like teeth, like claws
scratching, tearing,

his cry high and shrill,
like my child's, caught in a blackberry bramble.
Face stained with fury, Pop shakes his head. Trapped,
I can't wrench my father free.

Jig-Saw Puzzle ❧

You can build a man, piece by piece,
fit bulge into curve, match the blue of his overalls,
the S of his back, shoulders hunched. You can build

a whole town, gray thunderheads in the distance,
water tower above ochre leaves, the stretch of Main Street—
Irene's Café, Mobil station, Murphy's Hardware, shiny green

John Deere tractor parked in front, pavement rain-streaked,
a Chevy sedan—two-tone, turquoise and white—rushing, yet
suspended in time. Warning: Not intended for children under 3.

But say your Malamute tail-wags into the table. Say
your child under 3 shakes the legs. Say you step off the curb,
the two-tone Chevy rushing toward you. Say glaciers calve,

continents shift. Your world's in 1,000 pieces,
cardboard dust in the air.

Late November Woods ❧

Everything's dead. The aspen and oak slant
toward a lower sun
                   sap flow slowed,

bone-thin limbs stripped bare,
like your arms
                   reaching for someone

no one else sees, fingers so cold,
cold as the ground
                   now holding you.

Twisting in the wind, branches whisper
half-words
                   words left unsaid.

I wander alone through leaded-glass woods,
the forest floor
                   shadow-streaked,

black lines broken with light. No longer green,
the space between the trees opens.
                   Beyond –

distant mountains. The ridgeline, a body reclined
turns away
                   leans into sky.

Elegy in Autumn Fields ❧

He rips the engine back to life, straps
the brush-cutter to his chest. Balancing its heft
in gloved hands, he braces his legs against
the hillside behind their home, stumbles

through scrub, stubbled with rocks and stumps
hidden beneath dead leaves. The blade slashes
bramble, sapling, hobblebush; tears
bittersweet, thistle, the frost-withered

fronds of ferns; flings aster into the wind.
A flurry of seed stings his face. The air torn
with engine's roar, he swings the cutter
back and forth, a steady sweep down the hill.

At the bottom, he lets the throttle go. Shaft still
harnessed to his chest, he spits out bits of brush,
wipes his glasses clean, and, with the same rag,
mops his brow—
                                    this is good work,
this clearing away before winter takes hold.

Weather Report ❧

She hurtles through darkness down I-93, flips on the radio:
Possible early morning sleet. Elsewhere, wildfires blaze
in southern California. Tornadoes in Ohio. And,
it's hailing diamonds on Jupiter.

Somewhere far beyond her blue Subaru, somewhere
in our solar system's dark, a million carbon molecules,
frenzied by solar wind, pulsate to a frantic beat,
collide and, struck by lightning, plummet
through Jupiter's rings, compress and burn
to soot, soot to graphite, graphite
to diamond—a hailstorm
of diamonds, dazzling in the glint of a distant sun.
Far beyond I-93 it's hailing diamonds,

and in the morning rush, the sleet begins.
Her headlights spark the icy particles—
diamonds everywhere.

II

Blood Knot ❧

Cleaning out the shed, I find my father's tackle box,
tin painted camouflage-green, now a collage
of chipped paint, dents, blossoms of rust.
I untie the frayed cord serving as hasp,
slip my hand through the metal handle—a perfect fit
for my father's fingers, too large for mine—pry open
the lid, stiff hinges creaking along its spine,
and release the faint smell of canvas and fish,
that metal-against-metal scrape, the box sliding
beneath his seat at the canoe's stern.
My hand trembles as I lift each piece: the stringer,
a jangle of metal clips chained together; True Value sack
filled with snaps and swivels; bright bobbers; the lure
my father called "Joe" with yellow eyes and triple hook;
a velvet-lined box cradling beads and tear-drop spinners linked
to rusty hooks; and at the bottom, a weight tied to a blood knot—
line joined to line, the ends in his teeth as he tightens the knot.
I feel the hook's bite and the slow, steady tug as my father
reels me through dark water.

Cold ❧

I climb out my bedroom window,
crunch through snow in doe-skin slippers.
Winter tugging my nightgown,
I huddle within the boney arms
of brittle lilac bushes, wait
for my parents to discover I'm gone.

She'll come back when she gets cold enough.

They never knew how cold I was—
even before I ran away.

Quarrel 🍃

My parents never argued. No raised voices,
shouts. No angry words.

Instead, my mother would excuse herself
from the table, clear away the dirty dishes,

knives and forks, the empty glasses,
retreat to her kitchen.

It was the counter that bore her anger.
Setting her jaw, she shook

clotted cleanser onto linoleum, clenched
a rag, pressed down. She scoured

stains, old cuts, black mold along the edges.
Scrubbed until her hands burned.

Scoured and scrubbed again, then rinsed
the surface. Blood, grit, bacon grease,

the smell of garlic washed away
with terrycloth.

Better now.
But never clean enough.

Mother Tries to Teach Me a Proper Place Setting ❧

She places knife, spoon, fork
on our kitchen table, spoon and knife
to the right, fork to the left.

Flatware, like a family. The spoon,
my mother—round, stainless, no edge
at all. Concave, she reflects the world
upside down. The knife, my father—
thin, straight and unbendable.
His smooth edge faces my mother,
sharp edge and pointed remarks
aimed at the fork.
On the wrong side of the plate,

I'm on my own, spikes up, prickly,
ready to poke at peas, mash brown sugar
into sweet potatoes, twirl ribbons of spaghetti
into bows and twisty snakes.

I set the table, plunk spoon and knife
to the right, fork to the left. Metal on wood—
a leaden sound. My mother nods.

                        Someday,
when I have silver of my own, I'll bundle them
close together, in a linen napkin, touching,
and bind them with, maybe,
a strand or two of feather grass.

Mie O Kiru ❧

The woodblock print hangs in my father's study—
a Kabuki actor, noted for stage combat,
as samurai suspended in classic *mie* pose,
over-drawn frown carved on his face, one hand
overhead, fingers fanned and rigid, the other
gripping the sheath of his sword, ready.
If you look closer—old kimono
over old kimono, the dark, outer one flows open,
reveals the inner, patterned with yellow moths,
and a second sword.
Bare feet planted wide, body bent forward,
the old samurai narrows his eyes, stares
into a gold background, grass-writing scrawled
all around him.

Out the study window, my mother and I see
that same startled look—
my father in dark bathrobe and yellow-stained
pajamas, patterned with moth holes,
staring in the distance, a frown creasing his face.
Bare feet planted wide, body bent forward,
he grasps a metal garden rake with both hands.
He is frozen for that moment, the air dusted
with gold light, low, almost fading.
My father on stage,
dusk creeping into his rock garden, casting
shadows on dwarfed trees, miniature waterfalls,
rounded stones planted in swirls, five golden
koi finning in a pond.

Soft whispers in the *sasa* grass, chittering,
the scratch of raccoon claws on stone—
a masked intruder skulks through grasses,
washes greedy paws in pond water.

                                 AaaaaEeeeee!
A deep guttural wail. My father breaks pose, swings
his rake overhead, slashes air, strikes again,
again, metal teeth biting water lily,
grass, patterns of stone.   Sparks.
The clang of metal on rock.

Behind the study window, we witness
what would be an early scene
in the final act of his play.
My father, an old samurai raging at the night,
dark kimono flapping open—
and that masked intruder
stealing through shadows on small feet.

Wake (n.) ❧

Old Norse, *vok*, hole in the ice.
The Viking longship, dragon's prow lunging
forward, cuts through sea ice.
Long journey home—
narrow fjord, frigid shores, mountains
scowling at the sea.

Wave pattern generated by a boat knifing
across a lake. Shock waves compressed
in a wedge-shape, disturbance
spreading outward from its source.

Consequences of a destructive event—
tornado, hurricane, war.
The damage a father might leave.

A collection of buzzards.
Disturbed air, dark intentions spiraling down
to the dead.

Night vigil. My sisters cried, not my mother.
I peered over the casket rim. All shiny inside—
a white satin bed and Bapa Vic
wearing slick black suit, hair greased back,
silver ripples on satin.

What he left behind. A pattern of disturbance—
fiery outbursts, the red-head, doors slammed,
broken bottles, followed by silence, broken
wife, his child left to pick up the pieces.

He taught my mother to swim—
threw her overboard, rowed away.
She never forgave him, even in death—
Bapa Vic, laid out with hatchet and shield,
rides the Dragon Ship through a hole in the ice.

Bread ❧

Head bowed over a deep, earthen bowl,
my mother sifts flour, folds in salt,
oil, yeast, *goodness and mercy*
in small measure, and water,
warm over her wrist,
warm as blood.

Pressing against a floured board, she kneads
the dough, pushing away with heel of her hands,
pulling back, kneading, needing, *forever*
and ever pushing, pulling, rounding
and heeling, *deliver us from evil*,
pushing, pulling and
healing. *Deliver us.*

The dough, covered, sprinkled with water,
rests, rises in a warm place, *forgive us*
our trespasses, rests,
rises again.

She shapes the risen dough
into loaves, bakes them, her kitchen full
of the smell of her mother's kitchen—
surely goodness and mercy
should have followed all the days of her life.
Forgive me my trespasses. But not the one
who trespassed against her.

She lifts the bread from her oven, taps
each crown. *Thy will be done.*
A hollow sound.

Give us this day. That's all she asks for.
Nothing more. *I shall not want.*
I shall not

Rust 🍃

Given time, iron will turn to rust.
We drank well water the color of rust when I was little.
It tasted like blood in the back of my mouth.
Iron in the water my father said.

We drank well water the color of rust when I was little—
old well, metal parts, metal at its heart.
Iron in the water my father said.
He drove his Dodge sedan too many winters—

old car, metal parts, metal heart.
Beside him, I'd stare at the corroded hole beneath my feet,
his Dodge sedan driven too many winters.
I was afraid of falling through.

Beside him, I'd stare at the corroded hole beneath my feet,
a rainbow corona surrounding nothing, nothing at all.
Afraid of falling through,
I'd watch the road rush past.

A rainbow corona surrounding nothing, nothing at all,
my father now sits in the passenger seat of my rental car.
He watches the road rush past,
corrosion creeping up his spine, eating holes in his mind.

My father sits in the passenger seat—
osteoarthritis, advanced Alzheimer's,
corrosion creeping up his spine, eating his mind.
Do I know you? he asks.

Osteoarthritis, advanced Alzheimer's.
We return to a locked ward, memory care.
I stare at him. Do I know you?
His face frozen, limbs rigid.

He returns to his locked ward—memory suspended,
internal bearings rusted.
Face frozen, limbs rigid,
my father had an iron will.

Bearings rust.
The taste of blood in the back of his mouth,
my father had an iron will,
but, given time, iron turns to rust.

III

River-Walker

Below zero several days in a row. Half-crazy,
we dare each other to walk the frozen river.
Grabbing sticks, we slide down the bank
through knotweed tangle, hobblebush, snow,
poke at the surface, then step onto ice.
Before us, the river's back, long and sinuous,
milky white like quartz. Its mottled sky-gray
ridges—patterns of current and wind.

At first we test our footing, jab with sticks,
then, bolder, stride along its frozen spine,
ice snapping and groaning beneath our boots.
At the bend—boulders and deadfall,
brittle rings around the rocks, crackle-glaze,
and bubbles pushing against glass.
Beneath the cold, white surface, black water rages.
We come too close.

                    Even now,
sometimes I feel I'm walking on river ice,
hear that low, hollow moan—the sound
before the crack.

The Jays 🌿

It began as a kindness,
nights and days well below freezing,
snow covering the ground.
Before breakfast, I'd lay a handful
of peanuts on my deck. I remembered
my mother scattering nuts and seeds,
calling the jays.

And they came. At first only one.
A flash of blue, he stood before my offering
in crested hat, suit edged in white, a neat
black collar at his throat.
Cocking his head, he picked up the nut
in his beak and flew away.

Word spread. By the end of the week—
a mob of jays, all bravado and strut,
descends on the meager feast
with wild squawks, scolding and
hawk-imitations meant
to intimidate. They swagger
and brawl, flap their wings, peck
and shove at each other, grab
what they can get.

Chickadees, banished to the oaks, witness
the fray, as I do from my window.
One last raucous squawk and they're off—
only feathers and broken shells left behind.

In Front of Everyone

Behind a brittle smile, you shove
slow, pointed words at me.
Flushed cheeks, fingers trembling,
you hold your anger—
a hornet cupped in your hands.
Afraid to keep it, afraid
to let it go.

After They Quarrel ❧

Another blizzard on its way, he sets out to push back
chest-high snowbanks along their drive,

clear space for more. But nights of sleet, melt-freeze
have hard-packed the snow to ice. Three strokes—

his shovel breaks. Beard grizzled with frost,
he grabs a metal garden spade, thrusts it into

the frozen wall. Ramrod strokes, he jabs again,
again, splits the ice, shards flying; then

plants his legs, drives the spade into cracks, pries
ice chunks free, hurls them over the bank.

He kicks another with his boot, chucks it away.
And when he's done, stands back,

scans the broken snowbanks—
plenty of room for what's to come.

One Horse in a Paddock of Snow ❧

Facing the wind, she watches
the cows cluster in the distant field,
nose to nose, soft muzzle
and nudge, a collective breath rising
warm in the winter air.
Stable blanket strapped to her back,
the horse stands, watching company
she cannot keep.

Clear Cut

Once woods,
this hillside scoured, scraped,
furrowed with chain-laced skidder tracks—
brown scars in ashen snow

stubbled with stumps, bramble, alder,
the only green—feathery sprays of hemlock
too small to cut

littered with granite boulders, fallen snags,
sawdust, a stone wall spine,
woodchips, torn limbs
and tops of trees tossed into brush piles,
gray ghost-leaves shivering in a cold breeze

gutted, like a carcass picked over by crows,
hollow space beneath the ribs,
heart removed.

Dark-eyed Junco

It lies on my doorstep belly up,
breast pale, twig-feet perched on air,
slate-hooded head tilted to the side,
a smear of down and blood on the windowpane.

Moments ago, a trill of tickering notes,
flash of flint wingbeats hurtling
toward birch   limb-tangle   clouds   light
splinters   startling blue   body larger
larger   filling dark eyes   glass—

the self so clearly seen
just before the end.

Angels in the Snow ❧

Your body surrenders to gravity, falls
almost in slow motion, backwards
into drifts of new snow—
cold and glittering with light.
Earthbound, you fling your arms and legs
wide as possible, sweep back and forth,
again, create wings, a gown,
then struggle to stand without reaching back
and look at the image you've created—
your body's mold, the empty space left behind.
Maybe that's all we are: brief impressions
to be filled in tomorrow, or trampled
by hunters, the hooves of deer,
later to melt,
seep deep into the ground,
mingle with lacy litter
of last year's leaves.
Maybe that's all
we are.

Rough Road Ahead ❧

Just as snow begins to melt, just when you think
winter's past,
orange signs bloom beside the road: *Frost Heaves.*
Bump.
You notice small fissures at first, like creases pursed
at the edge of your lips,
not frown lines yet, just worry signs, a warning
of what's to come.
Ice masses beneath the surface thicken, swell, push
against pavement.
Once smooth, now humped and hollowed.
Upheaval followed
by collapse. Crevices snake through asphalt,
scars oozing
snowmelt, sand. Eyes to the road, I shift into low,
try to swing wide of the worst.

Broken Mailbox along Route 3A ❧

The gray metal mailbox
still dangles from its rear chain,
front rusted through—
a lop-sided swing, at odds
with the wind, red plastic flag
tight at its side.

Its door gapes open
to the snowbank below—
dirty snow, pock-marked,
crusted with sand, soot,
exhaust.

The postman
doesn't stop anymore.

Winter Koan

The only sound in the winter woods—
brittle beech leaves shivering
in the wind, clinging to branches
like paper prayers.

What moves?
Is it the leaves,
or the wind—the unseen current
between the leaves?
Perhaps the spirits of deer brushing past,
no longer needing woodland browse.
Or is it the winter mind of the listener?

North Country ❧

It's a harsh landscape   stern father, cold mother
my wool scarf wrapped three times, knotted at my throat
I break trail through crusted snow   shadow-streaked

strewn with torn branches   deep boot prints left behind
hidden streams rush below ice-layers   whispers, shushings
snuggle with my sister beneath blankets   *warm bedroom closet*

braiding stories, whispers   *shushhhhh! Pop's home*
coyote tracks crisscross with deer, sometimes align   hunger
and flight etched in white   *I run away*   *hide in winter wood*s

but no one comes   *when you're cold enough*
you just go home   granite rocks hunch beneath the frozen crust
never sure where to step   *I leave for good*   *leave my sister*

my mother finds her curled beside a snowbank   *waiting to die*
the trees, the stream   the bear in its wintry den   she
only seemed dead

I have run away for years   but born of north woods
I've come home   my roots spread outward
hold my trunk   silvered and scarred   firm

I am the beech   my rice-paper leaves persist through winter
thin prayers tied to limbs   my voice, a dry whisper
                 rattles in the wind.

IV

Winter Burn ❧

       a buried fire
is not always dead
even when smothered with snow

fire can burn inward
sear down through stumps
     travel deep underground
along roots, surface
        in unexpected places

its smell in your hair
your skin, the wool jacket you wore
days later—
        sometimes years

Thanksgiving ❧

November rainclouds roll back,
edges gold-stained with dying light—
pale blue beyond.

Beech leaves, parchment dry,
refuse to fall, shiver
on a sudden breeze.

A loon—then only a ripple.
Beneath the cold surface,
she dives into the lake's heart.

Mourners gather on the shore.
Behind us, in this mist-shrouded marsh,
winterberry offers red fruit.

Resting Place ❧

Through morning's silvered mist, we carry shovel, rock
from their garden and the velvet pouch—his ashes
in a cardboard box. Mother finally has her say,

chooses their own back woods, not that northern campsite,
that lake five hundred miles away—as he'd wanted.
She leans on my sister's arm. Then, jaw set, eyes bright,

she strikes off through wet grass grown long, leading us past
the gardens gone-to-seed and the old maple, now
just a stump, past yard's edge and into the thicket,

overrun with whips and saplings, blackberry canes.
We stumble through nettle and briar, thorns tearing
our sleeves. Bent low, feeling for solid footing, she

picks her way through leafy dark to wooded hill—and,
grabbing a branch to steady herself, she reaches
the fallen tree rubbed smooth with sitting, their sitting,

where after a day's work, they would rest and whisper
shushing sounds, speak to the birds. My sister and I
dig a hole, plant my father in soil black with silt,

leaf and decay. Earth, ash, bloodroot, the rock on top.
We hold hands in this green place, hear the forest breathe—
hush of wind, leaf-sigh, a white-throated sparrow's cry.

From the shadows, a buck takes shape—antlers branching,
head high. Unmoving, still, he stares at us, eyes dark
as night, before passing into the yawning light.

Each morning from their porch, my mother hears his call,
the sparrow's high insistence—here, here, here.

Peeling an Apple ❧

She pulls the knife closer, blade flat
against the fruit, small cuts, a steady rhythm,
turning the apple as she works, paring
from base to stem, a circular path—
the thin layer of skin,
one long ribbon

        spiraling down, the curled uncurling,
a fiddlehead coiled tight, unwinding, the samara
wind-whirling toward the ground, a veery
unreeling its song, one note descending
into another, never-ending, maples
twisting as they grow, faraway
galaxies spinning, worlds like,
unlike ours.

The part she loves best
she throws on the compost heap for the deer to eat,
or to decompose within that dark, and
return to earth—a new beginning,
its circular path.

T'ai Chi in a Winter Storm

crown-point lifted   my feet press into the floor
arms rise   reach forward

toward frenzied flurry   snow and sleet
wind-flung waves   rattle my windowpane

palms push down   body sinks   slows
arm arches into a bow   warding off

the arctic roar   icy bite   bitter winds
snarl and rage   treetops bend

roll back   bird's tail beyond my grasp
ravens   black brushstrokes   swirl in white

circle waist   single whip   follow
winds whipping   sweeping the earth

sweeping heaven   white crane spreads its wings
snowflakes feather   flurried flight

hushing   brushing   brush knee   push
clouds roll open   close   around me

body moving   mind still   be like winter

Release ❧

From a single point, particles explode—
seeds of stars, planets, moons hurled into the dark.

Mount St. Helen's, Vesuvius, Fuji.
Earth's heart erupts, spews layer on layer,
lava and ash. Cinder to glass. The inner
now outer crust.

A steady stream cooled my father's molten rage,
dementia slipping into sleep.
His bony fingers grasped my hand.
Wouldn't let go.

The oak holds its leaves into November.
Yellow turns to brown. Then, a windless day—
the leaves just fall,
turn over and over, drift
through gray.

Wings unhinged, a hundred doves burst
from a wicker basket. Clamor for flight, for light.

I didn't cry at my father's funeral.
Months later, snowmelt off the mountain,
I cannot stop.

Summers ago, a shutter opened, captured a moment—
Pop in his buffalo plaid holding a fish.
Now, only the buffalo plaid exists.
My son wears it in his garden.

Witch hazel, gorse, touch-me-not.
Along a seam of vulnerability, pods split,
fling seeds at the sky.

Long time-lapse at night, my camera traces
trails of stars—circles coursing outward
from a single point.

Return to Magnetic Rock, Northern Minnesota ❧

Only charred skeletons remain along the path
we used to hike. Black trunks scrape the sky,
pinecones clenched on charcoal limbs.
When I was little you held a cone,
told me for the seeds to sprout the tree must burn.
Now, these seeds and ashes mingle
in this once-woods. Stone cairns mark the trail
across raw outcrops ribboned with shale and Indian flint.
Beyond—exposed ridgelines, snag-stubbled.
And beneath it all, a wash of green.

From a high ledge, I see it—
the glacial erratic rising like an ancient standing stone.
I pick my way down,
past shafts of dead trees into the hollow below.
From ashen soil, blueberry bushes crowd everywhere.
Jack pine seedlings brush my knees.

As I near it, my compass needle spins,
then steadies. North points to Magnetic Rock.
The boulder towers above me—
a lodestone holding old stories: continental rift,
shifting poles, the north of another time.
I press my hand along its fractures, scars
forged by the crush of ice; feel the steady pull,
one body toward another.
Wind stirring through young pine, I hear you
whisper my name.

Tinder

Dead twigs, brittle pine needles,
bark, crumpled newspaper
tied in a knot,

my heart.
It takes so little—
the strike of a match, soft breath,

your touch—
to turn what was cold
into flame.

V

Ice-Out on Newfound Lake 🌿

A thin layer persists, melt-freeze cut
by the wind's brushstroke, the crisscross
of old snowmobile trails. A calloused surface,

shirred, translucent like a snakeskin.
Wrapped in a restless wind, I watch oak leaves
brittle-skitter across the lake. Sky in pools,

crows sip clouds underfoot. Along the edge,
an icy slurry shivers—broken glass shifting.
I've been here before, winter weary,

dark months behind. Perhaps it's enough
to know there will be no great crack, no
splintering heave. Only thaw and letting go.

What had been frozen so long
just grows soft, sloughs off its skin.
Waterways zigzag through ice, seams

opening to all that's hidden below—
tangled weeds, mud, emerging life.
And in the distance, mist lifts, seeping light.

Crane Fly

I wake to a crane fly beating
against my windowpane.
Fooled by transparency,
it beats again and again.
An untidy knot—
gray, slender body pulsing,
long legs, like thread,
splayed in all directions, trembling,
veined wings fluttering.

Turn around!
The mist is rising over Newfound Lake.
You have only this day. Fly
into the astonishing world behind you.

It stutter-stitches across
the cold morning glass.
Then back again.

Coriolis Effect ❧

Over great distances, long periods of time, moving objects
veer off-course.

Half a world away, you search, find my name, remember
half a lifetime ago, a semester abroad
reading Tennyson and Keats.

Once, in a field of primrose, violet, forget-me-not,
I woke in your arms, sky larks trembling overhead.

If a pendulum swings in free flow,
its path rotates clockwise, marking the passage of time.

You want to see me. Will fly anywhere to meet.
My pulse quickens.
Long-forgotten longing.

If a pilot flies a straight line from London to LA,
he will curve right, never reach his mark.
He must constantly correct for the Earth's turn.

The same moon has risen each night over me
that rose, hours before, over you.
But the moon grows old.
So do we.

I'm married now. My son in college. A dog.
A husband who works too much.

What happens when high pressure systems collide with low?
Cyclonic flow spins out of control.
Irene, Katrina, the Angry Red Spot of Jupiter.

You sit across the table; talk about what you've done.
Not done.

All I see are your shoulders slumped,
vein-webbed cheeks too red.

A moth's flight—hunter in the night. Vibrating hairs sense
the turns as it dives through air.

But the Earth has turned too many times. Moving objects
veer off-course.

I reach for the check, dog hair on my sleeve,
touch your hand as I leave.

Pas de Deux ❧

Suspended mid-air from a crane's tip,
    the climber swings to the pine

and, like a dancer, sweeps his arm around
    his partner's waist. Chain-saw dangling,

he bridles the top, lifts his saw, shifts weight
    and slices. Together, treetop and man

lower to the ground.

        Once more he's skyward—

balanced, sashing the trunk with a sling,
    he glides down, plants his feet and

cuts. Below, he steadies the pine's sway,
    guides it onto the truck bed. Bowing

his head, he holds tender limbs in his arms, eases
    them into the mulcher.

Woodchips burst in applause—
    the scent of Christmas everywhere.

Redbud ❧

Flamingo-beaked buds open on bare branches.
Pollen-drunk, the long-tongued bees
mount bright blossoms.
Startled,
petals burst pink against a blue sky.

Only after the gaudy show—
tender leaves, red-rimmed, unfold,
grow into a heart.

Vernal Pool ❧

The spring peeper's song rises, shivers like sleigh bells.
Wood frogs gabble-clatter, gabble-clatter. Then silence
as we near. Hidden beneath alder and winterberry

a pool quivers with the disappearance of frogs.
Speckled egg masses cling to twigs. Waving a stick, my son
stirs snowmelt, sodden oak leaves, silt. A dark world

tea-stained, full of startled life—three-tailed nymphs, scuds,
water scorpions darting through decay. He plunges
his hands into icy water. Fairy shrimp, translucent ghosts

slip through his fingers. I crouch beside him
as he splashes again and again, laughing at the tickle
of tails wriggling away. Water, mud, sunlight splatter

everywhere. And even as I watch, I feel this moment
shimmer through my fingers, like fairy shrimp—
no more than a flutter.

Trust ❧

Downy thump into glass—
a soft gray body trembles on my deck,
bobbing head, pulse at throat.

Eyelids blink, then close.
Behind the pane, I wait in stillness.
Soft breath, in and out.

I stood like this long ago, watching
my baby sleep. Who was I
to care for such a fragile thing?

Now, outside my window, my son
brushes off scuffed knees, climbs
on his bike, doesn't look back.

The phoebe shifts, twitches his tail,
lifts on twig feet—a balance point.
Cocking his head, he opens

his beak and mimes a cry.
I hold back the wanting to hold.
Blur of wings—

    then gone.
Squinting into light, I witness flight.

Monarch Butterflies on Joe-Pye Weed ❧

You cling to these late summer blossoms,
uncurl fine filaments, kneading,

needing sweet nectar. Hinged wings open,
close like ancient Chinese kites,

silk dyed tiger-bright, trimmed with black
calligraphic designs. You feed and flutter,

then lift, tilt in the air, set sail—fragile prayers
flying to the gods. *Safe journey.*

My Son Calls from Base Camp, High Andes ❧

Your fogged photo on my cell—
eyebrows and beard frosted, your smile,
Cotopaxi brooding over your shoulder. You always
looked up—falcons clinging to a ledge, jet trail carved
in the sky, now a snow-crusted volcano.

Your voice thin as the air you breathe.
Three miles high. Another half to go. I thread your words—
climb at midnight   glacier more stable   no sun to burn our eyes
headlamp   ropes link me   the guide   ice-axe up volcano's spine
broken glacier   chasm   snow-ladders across
frozen mist   dawn-smeared   touch the crater's rim   summit
descend before the glacier shifts

The night you were conceived, I dreamt I touched the sky—
obsidian smooth and cold, fiery glints sparking the black.
I wanted to pluck a star. But, even in my dream
I knew what every mother knows,
you can't hold fire in your hand.

Signal breaks. My ground shifts. I cradle your voice, press
the image of you, headlamp aimed at the sky,
tight against my heart.

Meteorite

1

Holding hands beneath their worn bed-quilt,
they lean back in lawn chairs, watch shards
of light streak the night sky. A fireball flares,
hissing, spitting red and gold sparks,
a trail of glitter behind—
touches earth.

2

Within a ceremonial kiva—
a star-stone,
smooth and black as night, silver-tinged,
wrapped in sage and feather robe.
A winged creature that can no longer fly.

3

An unearthly chime. His hoe rings against rock,
half-buried in loam, heaved up by spring frost.
The man levers it free, tugs it from the ground and,
eying its size, its heft, its charred surface mottled
with strange indents, he lugs it home to show his wife.
She sets it on the kitchen floor, props the door open,
lets in a warm breeze. And lilacs.

4

Dark pebble in desert sand,
its ancient feel old as the sun.
She binds it with a silver chain
to wear at her throat.

5

The gods have been known to descend
into our world—a flash of fire, then dark flight,
their bright light hidden
beneath a cap and muslin shirt.
To touch a woman's hand, the pulse
at her throat, to smell lilacs, sage—
they choose earth.

Bloodroot

Pale, leathery leaf, lobed
like the palm of my hand, clasps
a slender stem, artery-red,
with single white flower—
the first each spring to push through snow
and the fetid forest duff behind my house.

My mother always knew where to find them
in her Minnesota woods. I remember her
kneeling, pushing back leaf litter,
uncovering the plant. To show me
its secret, she picked the flower.
Red sap bled in her hand.
Was it dead?

What I couldn't see—the rhizome
buried beneath the earth, branching out,
connecting one to another,
living still.
The next spring, the next, even in these woods
years after my mother's death,
the bloodroot will bloom again—
and bleed.

emptiness 🌿

dark
between the stars
the Dipper ladles night

leaves shiver
where an owl once was

wind breathes through pines

white space
paints a picture
around the poet's words

air trembles
through a narrow flute

from emptiness song

VI

I look into the lake— 🦋

woods and sky look back

the way an owl vanishes into oak,
gray feathers, gnarled bark, shadows

and flickered light, its call—wind whickering
through woods, or the way a toad flattens

on dead leaves, legs splayed, body curved
to a tip, bright leaf-rib striped down its back,

or a pike weaves through eelgrass and weed,
waves of green, sun-speckled side, belly sand.

Body takes its form from place.
                          Feet rooted in earth,

storm and still, snowmelt and summer rain
seeping through my veins, my body bends

with the wind, eyes flickering grey green,
winter clouds braided in my hair.

Shelter in Place

An open cup, the size of my hand,
rootlets and fiber, snips of string
woven in a twig's fork,

oak roots, gnarled, exposed,
moss clustering within each V—
a galaxy of green stars,

dead tree, the space between
loose bark and heart—
a many-chambered cavern for beetles,
ants, long-nosed borers,

cave in a south-facing cliff, overhanging
rock, a few sticks and fluff, hollow log,
a scrape in the sand, fur-lined tunnels
nuzzling through earth, deep
river hole,

       and for me—a granite floor,
carpet of needle and loam,
tall red-pine walls, shingled bark
and the night sky—
              a billion fires burning

Degrees of Freedom

Head tilted back, you watch a pair of falcons
circle and dive, flash slate-gray. I bend close
to the rock, touch blossoms
of gold lichen. The granite holds us,
shoulder leaning into shoulder,
in its sun-warmed palm.

Nested in my loft, I scribble
words on lined paper. Below,
the crack of a maul
as you split wood in the snow
for our evening fire.

Three thousand miles away, surrounded
by stippled cliffs, the dusky roar of ocean,
I sketch anemones with my sister,
feed a campfire on the beach.
In the distance, birds I don't know
call your name.

He holds me close, swaying
to a blues beat. But
it's in your arms I wake each morning,
your breath a slow dance
on the back of my neck.

The trellis between us, grapevine splayed
in opposite directions,
I see only your hands, calloused,
creased, stained magenta. Parting leaves,
you cup a cluster of ripe fruit.
I know these hands.

Still Life ❧

On our kitchen table—
earflaps unsnapped, your oil-skin cap roosts
on a stack of dog-eared Filson catalogues, a moon
phase chart and photos of the falcons in flight.

Binoculars, half out of their case, wait
beside a well-thumbed field guide, curved to the shape
of your hip, and your small, leather notebook—
goldfinches beginning to show bright yellow feathers—
the page held open with a round, black river-stone,
from a stream you like to fish, feet grounded
in quiet.

A pencil worn to a stub and a
crossword puzzle cut from last week's local paper,
block letters in each box. You've filled all
the empty spaces.

Snowfall ❧

—from Nazim Hikmet's "Things I Didn't Know I Loved"

1

Sitting in our window seat
I watch the first snow fall
flakes large and airy
suspended in this half-light
I never knew how much I loved
snow falling—such softness, generosity
the way it swirls and drifts almost in slow motion
settles over brittle curls of fern, withered leaves
the year is dying
aspen and birch the first to shed their leaves
late-blooming flowers, their seeds
the snow drifts on quiet flakes, like milkweed seed
do you remember the milkweed streaming above us
seeds spilling from dried husks
wind-blown and alive against the blue
the smell of crushed aster, sweat, the earth beneath us

2

I've always loved the earth
that fecund, half-rotting smell
dirt beneath my fingernails
my father gave each daughter a square of rich, black loam
I planted moss rose and coxcomb, pleat-petalled zinnias
a sunflower once
its head grew so big and heavy, its stem broke
my father's father tried to farm until the farming life broke him
in a good year, sunflowers stretched far as he could see
a million suns

once I saw Van Gogh's sunflowers—thick chips of paint
dried and broken, like land in drought
too many years of drought and pestilence
cutworms, long-horned weevils, things with chewing mouths
but my grandfather loved the fireflies
their larvae, worms that glowed, ate the eaters

3
I've always loved fireflies, too
I love to watch them rise slowly from the grass into the trees
that riotous blinking and blinking
they speak to each other in tongues we once knew
my sisters and I played with them when we were little
barefoot in the grass, we'd chase them
the fireflies would flicker mid-air, then disappear
if we were lucky, we might catch one
feel the tickle of wings and tiny feet in our cupped hands
then let it go
do you remember those nights in Afton
walking hand in hand
carrying a lantern through open fields and deep woods
we were the fireflies
feeling our way through the night and into the stars
sometimes it's hard to tell where fireflies stop and stars begin

4
I've always loved the stars
so bright they burn holes in the night
my mother told us the stories written on a night-sky wall
she liked the dark ones best—Andromeda chained to a rock

Perseus chopping off Medusa's head, her hair, writhing snakes
and from that blood, a flying horse rose into the sky
I pretended to ride that horse
strong, rippling flanks beneath my thighs
together we'd fly through a spray of stars
like those here on our mountainside
stars bright because of the dark
distant suns, perhaps no longer there
perhaps already burned out, turned to ash
their light streaming through time and cold space
sparks to our eyes
their light still alive

5

I've always known I loved the light
but I didn't know I also loved the dark
the patterns on our bedroom wall when the sun first rises
the tangled shadows of bittersweet in a vase
even the gray days
the long winter nights
the blanket they throw over our shoulders
and now, another winter begins
fifty winters we've passed together
I watch this first snow fall
hear you split wood for the fire
I love our evening fire, the sudden rush, the crackle
the leopard-spotted coals, their deep, burning glow
snow drifts on quiet flakes outside our window
I never knew how much I loved winter
I never knew how much I loved

Origami, Refolded ꕤ

Given a square of washi paper—mine
textured, stained earth shades and ash

I line up the edges, press sharp folds
on a hard surface, rotate, reverse,
turn over, under, over years into
mountains, valleys, crevices,
unseen ravines.

My paper worn, wrinkled, torn
along deep seams, edges softened,
I unfold, smooth the creases.
Light feathers through.

I begin again. A simpler shape—
paper wings, flight aligned
with the vast, dark Universe ever folding,
unfolding.

At the Edge of the Androscoggin ❧

monarchs tilt
on goldenrod and virgin's bower—
  fragile balance
on slender blades

  beneath the riffled surface
speckled trout face upstream
  holding against the current

a great blue heron startles
long legs push off
  heavy body rising
   above the twisted sedge—
  mirror image a wavering
watercolor shape

   I grow old with the sun
cast my light with a lower slant

feet pressing into cobble and sand
  I rise with slow wingbeats
   from the river's edge
touch earth heaven

swamp candles light my way home

Acknowledgments

Grateful acknowledgment to the readers and editors of the following publications in which these poems first appeared, sometimes in earlier forms.

Chapbook
Bloodknot (Porkbelly Press, 2015), "Blood Knot," "Cold" and "Rust"

Anthology
A Walk with Nature: Poetic Encounters that Nourish the Soul (University Professors Press, 2019), "Return to Magnetic Rock, Northern Minnesota"

Journals
Cider Press Review: "Along the Edge of the Mad"

EcoTheo Review: "Monarch Butterflies on Joe-Pye Weed," "Redbud," and "T'ai Chi in a Winter Storm"

Gyroscope Review: "Coriolis Effect" and "Ice-Out on Newfound Lake"

Heartwood Literary Magazine: "River-Walker"

Hummingbird: "Thanksgiving"

Oakwood: "Trust"

Red Coyote: Vermillion Literacy Project: "Quarrel"

riverSedge: A Journal of Art and Literature: "Degrees of Freedom"

Rockvale Review: "Front Porch" and "Late November Woods"

Sky Island Journal: "emptiness" and "Origami, Refolded"

Smoky Quartz: "Crane Fly"

SPANK the CARP: "Wake"

The Sow's Ear: "Winter Burn"

Tinderbox Poetry Journal: "Dark-eyed Junco"

Tule Review: "Angels in the Snow"

Twisted Vine Literary Arts Journal: "Meteorite"

Up North Literary Journal: "After They Quarrel," "Bloodroot," and "The Jays"

U.S. 1 Worksheets: "After Her Death" (retitled "Elegy in Autumn Fields")
Watershed Review: "Clear Cut," "Release," and "Vernal Pool"

Written River: A Journal of Eco-Poetics: "Reaching Equinox" (retitled "at the edge of the Androscoggin"), "Weather Report," and "Winter Koan"

My thanks to the many teachers who inspired and helped me grow as a poet, especially, most recently, my mentors at the Frost Place Conference on Poetry—Vievee Francis, Martha Rhodes, Matthew Olzmann, Patrick Phillips, Gabrielle Calvocoressi, and Ross White. Thanks as well to fellow writers in the Women of Words writing group—Jennifer Highland, a true friend who never flinches at giving insightful, honest feedback, Liz Ahl, who took me under her very nurturing wing, Kate Donahue, and Kathy Drexel.

I am especially grateful to Ginger Murchison, poet, editor, mentor, friend, for her loving support and wise guidance over the past decade. She saw the value of my work and generously taught me the many layers of craft I needed to shape that raw material into poetry. Thank you, Ginger!

Special thanks to Christine Cote, visionary and editor of Shanti Arts, who brought my work into the world, enriching it with her own artistic touch.

Also, I am grateful to my parents, who taught me to look closely at the natural world. And to Jim, my husband and First Reader, for fifty years of constancy and support and love, with enough degrees of freedom to write a book. And to Chris, my son, climber-of-mountains, bearer-of-joy.

And, of course, I give thanks every day to the greatest teachers of all—the woods and the lake and the mountains and all the many varied, marvelous beings within.

About the Author

 Suzanne Rogier Marshall is the author of *A Falling Leaf and Other Poetry Activities* (Learning Publications, 1983) and the poetry chapbook *Blood Knot* (Porkbelly Press, 2015). A Pushcart nominee, her poems have appeared in *The Eco-Theo Review, Sky Island Journal, SPANK the CARP, Cider Press Review, Tinderbox Poetry Review* and many other journals and anthologies. After teaching middle-school English for nearly forty years, Suzanne retired with her husband to the mountains of New Hampshire, where she draws inspiration for her writing.

CPSIA information can be obtained
at www.ICGtesting.com
Printed in the USA
LVHW080755080822
725387LV00004B/751

9 781956 056358